THE SECRET DIAGRAMS
OF MANTIS FIST

THE CULTURAL GUTTER
presents

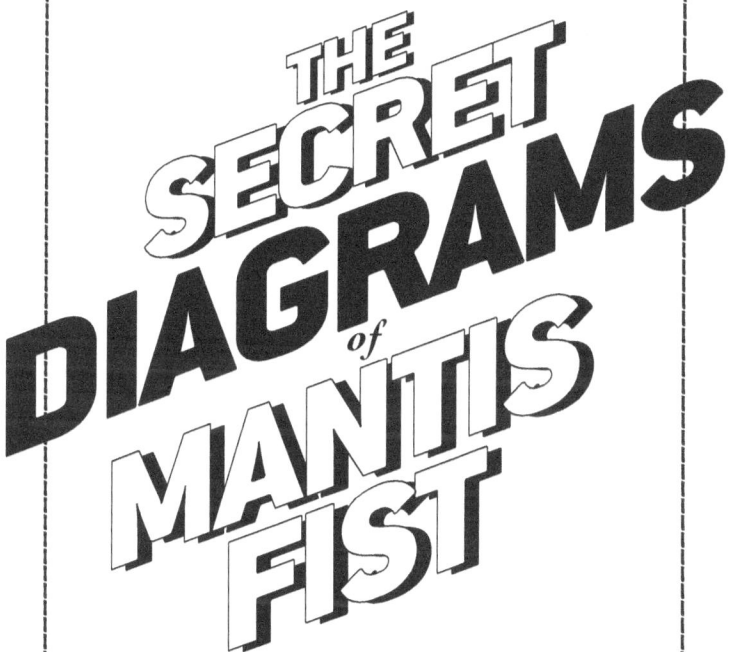

THE SECRET DIAGRAMS *of* MANTIS FIST

BY CAROL BORDEN

ILLUSTRATIONS BY EVAN MUNDAY

CULTURAL GUTTER **PRESS**

ISBN-13: 978-0692711170
ISBN-10: 0692711171

CONTENTS

Thanks

Thank you to Andrew Nahem for suggesting we make this book and then willingly designing it. Thanks to Evan Munday for his unbeatable illustration fist. Thank you to Colin Geddes for his Mantis Fist film suggestions. Thank you to the Cultural Gutter readers who made Mantis Fist diagrams in particular and kung fu training guides in general one of the most common and most perplexing search terms leading people to the Gutter. Thank you for repeatedly demanding on social media that we share our kung fu diagrams despite our having no kung fu diagrams, manuals, scrolls, pamphlets, mosaics or bas-reliefs. At least we didn't until this recent discovery.

INTRODUCTION

For years, readers of the Cultural Gutter have accused us of having manuals containing secret kung fu knowledge that we deliberately refused to admit to or share. In particular, readers believed we had a set of diagrams that would teach their possessors Mantis Fist style kung fu.

The Cultural Gutter is a website dedicated to writing about disreputable art, not to training students in secret martial arts. We did not understand how anyone could believe that we would have access to any kind of martial art diagrams, manuals, scrolls, books, oral traditions, mosaics or subterranean bas-reliefs. We denied it. We pointed to our many articles on other, non-martial subjects. We pointed out our own effete frailty and scholarly inclinations. And yet search terms related to these subjects continued to bring readers to the Cultural Gutter, readers hungry for knowledge of Mantis style kung fu given the prevalence of "Mantis Fist diagrams" as a search term. And we faced questions and even accusations on social media no matter how vociferously we denied the existence of any Cultural Gutter Mantis Fist diagrams. Sometimes, we feared that our denials only fueled our accusers' beliefs that we were keeping our martial art skills secret.

During recent maintenance work on the Cultural Gutter headquarters, a worker fell through a hole in the break room floor, discovering a secret chamber beneath CGHQ. Even more, we discovered in this vault, the skeletalized body of what could only be an antiquarian, a flashlight, a small wooden table and atop that table, a collection of diagrams. These diagrams are fragmentary in nature, but they are, in fact, illustrations of a set of Mantis Style kung fu forms.

Remarkably, we also discovered a second set of Mantis Fist diagrams that we believe has never been published or distributed in any manner before. We hope that you will be as excited about these discoveries are we are.

Carol Borden,
On behalf of the Cultural Gutter.

A Brief History of Mantis Fist Style Kung Fu

Mantis Fist was created by martial arts master Wang Lang in Shandong. There is some dispute about wether Wang created Mantis Fist during the Ming Dynasty (1368-1644) or the Qing Dynasty (1644-1912).

In the first version of the story, Wang created Mantis Fist during the Ming Dynasty, before a Manchurian invasion established a Manchurian emperor on the imperial throne. Wang traveled throughout the country mastering kung fu techniques to increase his own fighting skills. When he could defeat anyone who dared face him, he decided to challenge the monks of the Shaolin Temple, famous for their martial arts skills. The Shaolin monks were famous for their martial arts skills. It took Wang a long time to get the monks to pay any attention to his challenges, and when they finally did, they sent a novice to spar with him. Wang felt insulted, but he agreed, thinking once he defeated the novice, the monks would take him seriously and someone more appropriate would agree to fight him. The novice easily defeated him.

Astonished but not entirely discouraged, Wang went back home and concentrated on improving his fighting skills for two years. When he returned to Shaolin, he defeated not only the novice, but all the monks in the temple before facing the abbot himself. Then Wang lost again.

This time, Wang remained in the Lao Shan mountains, not far from the Temple. Determined to defeat the abbot and prove himself first in the martial world, Wang began training. This time, as he practiced, he happened to notice a praying mantis fighting a cicada. He was so impressed with the praying mantis's fighting skills, that he captured it and, using a small stick, he observed its responses to various attacks. After these observations, and presumably after releasing the mantis, Wang began working on replicating the mantis attacks and defensive moves. He added elements from other forms of kung fu that he had learned. Deciding he needed quick foot work, Wang added movements from Monkey Fist. When he felt his new style was perfected, Wang returned to the Shaolin Temple and defeated the abbot. Amazed, but always committed to learning, the abbot and the monks asked Wang to teach them this amazing style, but Wang refused.

Instead he left the temple and only taught select students his new style of kung fu, keeping his techniques secret for a long time. Alternatively, Wang created Mantis Fist during the Qing Dynasty. In this version, Wang traveled to the Shaolin Temple because it was a center of resistance to Manchurian rule. Wang wanted to help overthrow the Qing Dynasty and restore the previous Ming Dynasty. Unfortunately, while Wang was at the temple with the emperor accused the abbot of harboring rebels and ordered the Shaolin Temple burned. Wang fled and later met up with several monks, including senior monk Feng. They continued their martial arts studies (and presumably their Buddhist studies, but that is less important in this story).

Wang trained hard, but could never defeat his friend Feng. When Feng had to go on a monk duties-related trip for three years, he cheered up Wang by promising to duel him on his return. Wang immediately began working on his fighting skills.

As in the other version of the story, while training Wang observed a praying mantis fighting with a much larger cicada. He was impressed with the mantis' fighting and developed techniques based on his observation. When Feng returned, Wang easily defeated him. Wang and Feng then began perfecting the form and ultimately taught it to the Shaolin monks. Then the form was eventually taught to lay martial artists. As the tradition of Northern Mantis kung fu was passed along, practitioners continued to adapt it leading to many forms.

Regardless of what version of the story of Mantis Fist is correct, we, of course, know it was created based on a mix of deep understanding of the Shaolin martial arts and the observation of the mantis itself. Preferably by a martial arts master in the woods. The point is, though, that Mantis Fist was created to kick some Qing courtier ass and restore the Ming Dynasty.

DIAGRAM SET 1:
Northern Mantis Fist

The following diagrams depict eight stances of
Mantis Fist kung fu. While it doesn't represent
all the possible permutations of every style of
Mantis Fist, it is a good starting point.

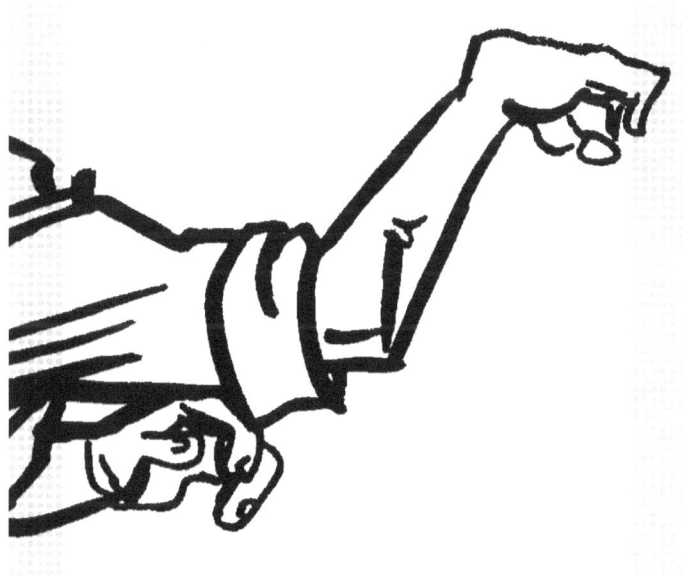

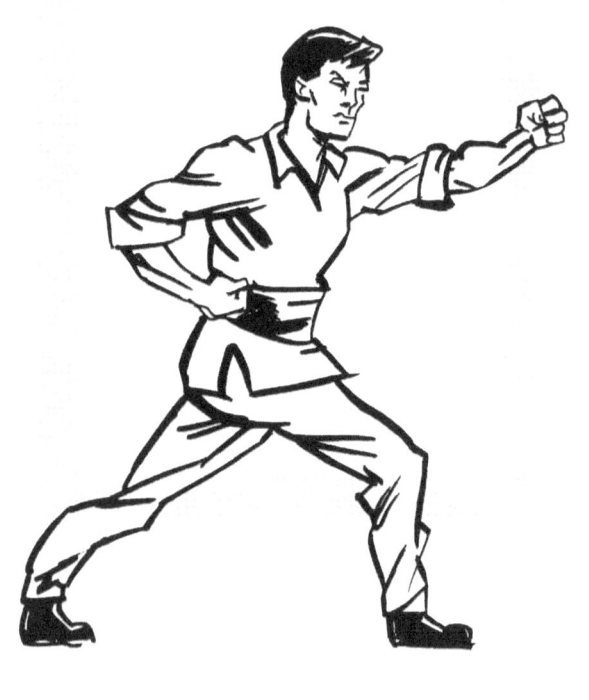

fig.1

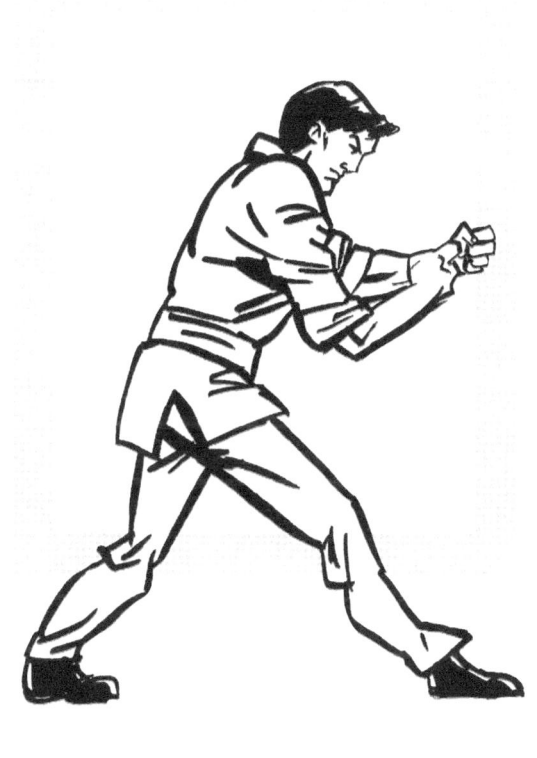

fig.2

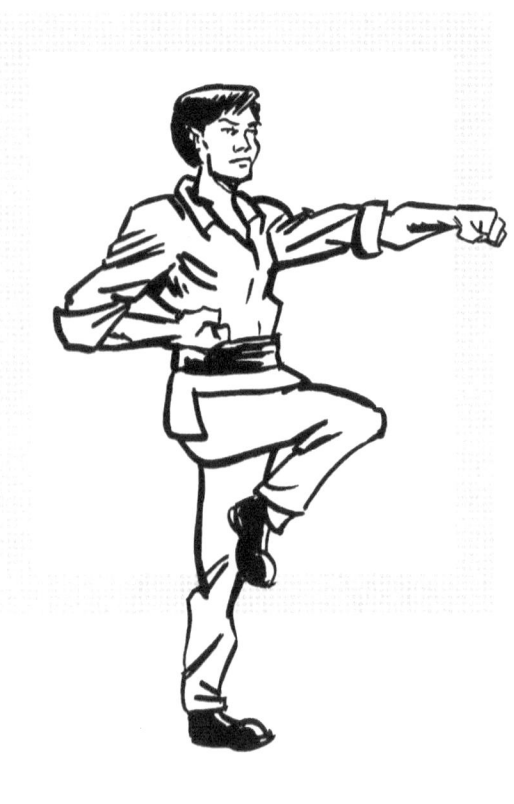

fig.3

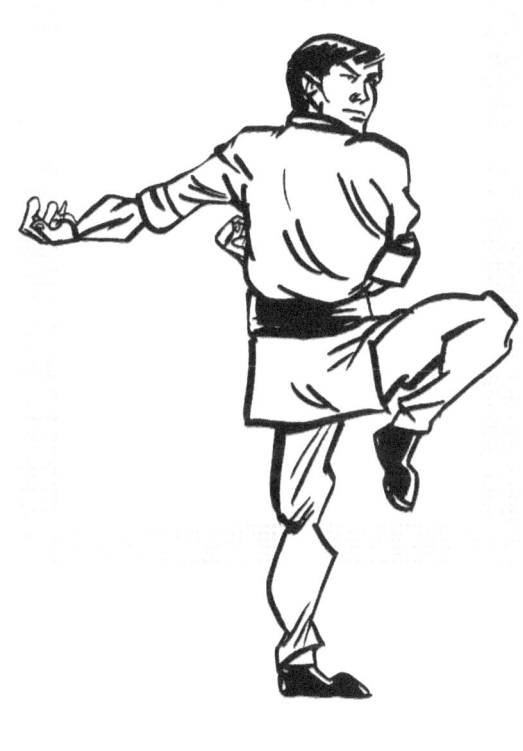

fig.4

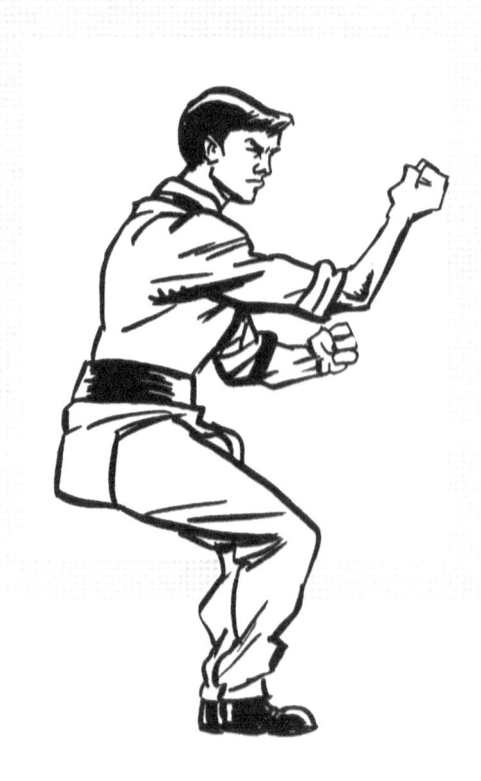

fig. 5

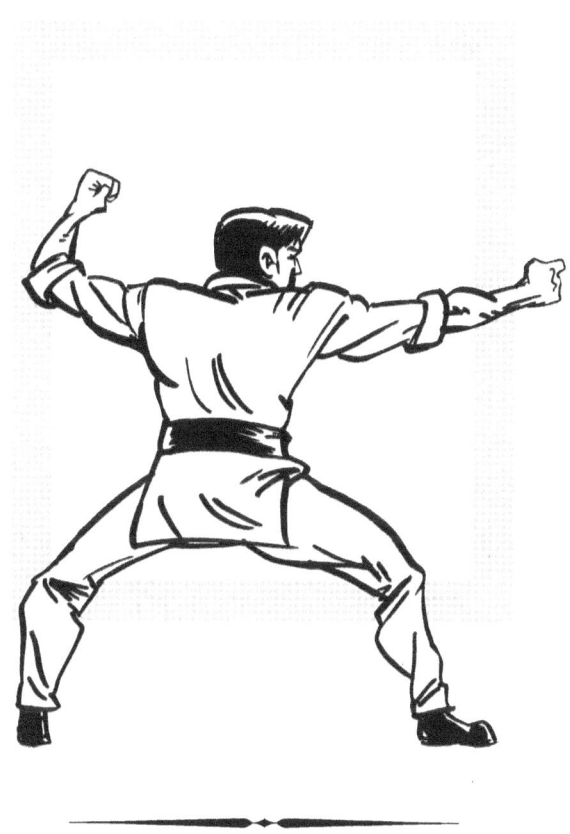

fig.6

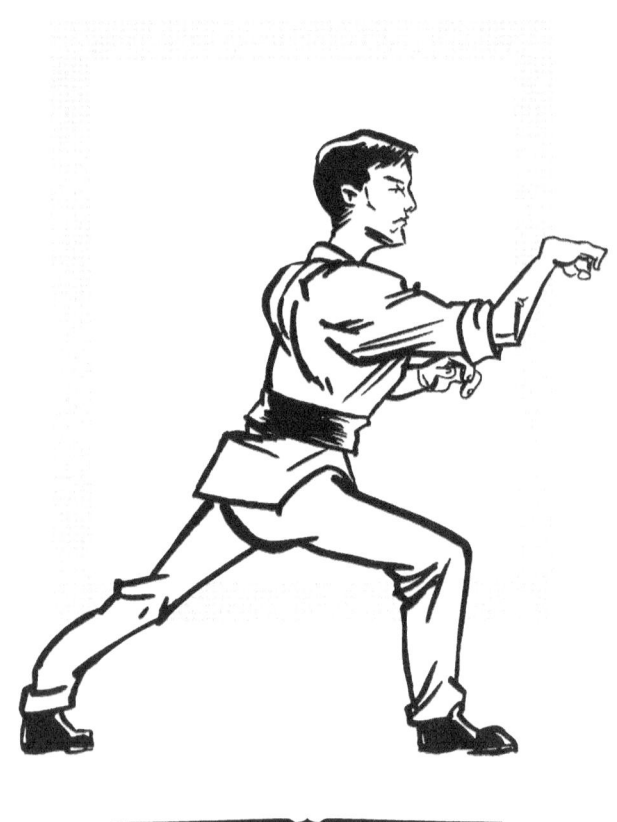

*fig.*7

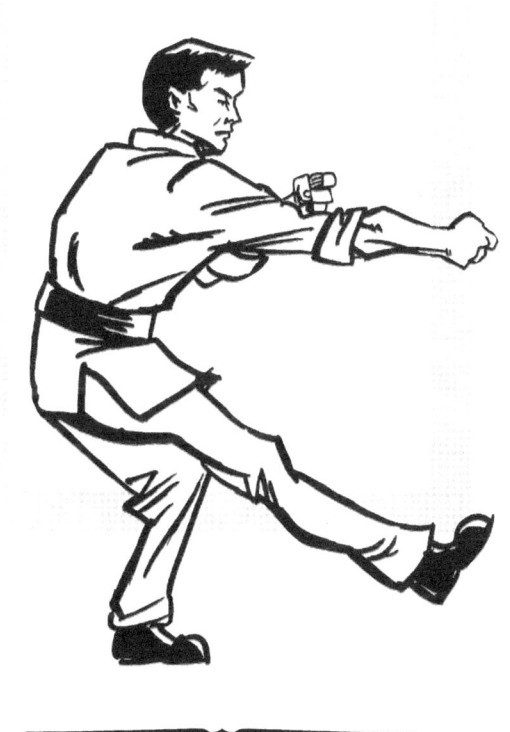

fig.8

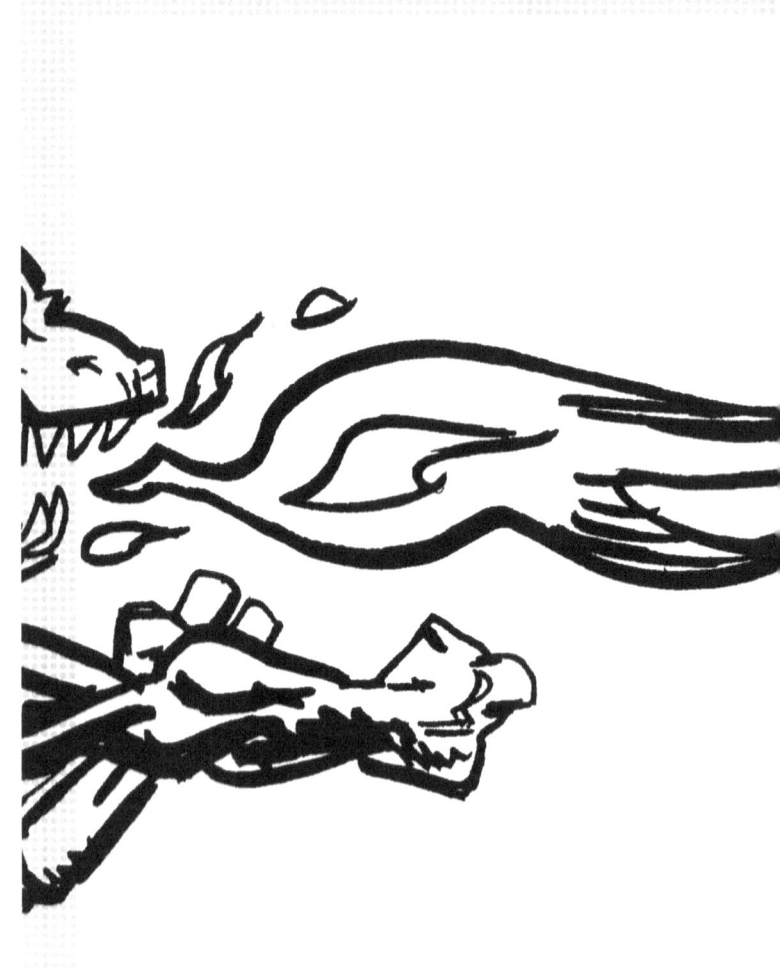

DIAGRAM SET 2:
Godzilla Kaiju Mantis Fist

Mixed among the more orthodox diagrams, we came across others that we cannot account for. They depicted a giant monster practicing Mantis Fist. We believe that this is the first publication of the Godzilla Mantis Fist Diagrams. However, it is possible that a Master of Mantis Fist observed a giant monster such as Godzilla in the wild and modified his techniques in order to improve his power and chi flow. It is also possible that Godzilla being partial to martial arts, as exhibited by his use of both sumo techniques and the No Shadow Kick, not to mention his clear interest in dueling other notable kaiju, had himself mastered the Northern Mantis Fist Style and modified it to suit his size and physiognomy. Most notably his tail and atomizing breath.

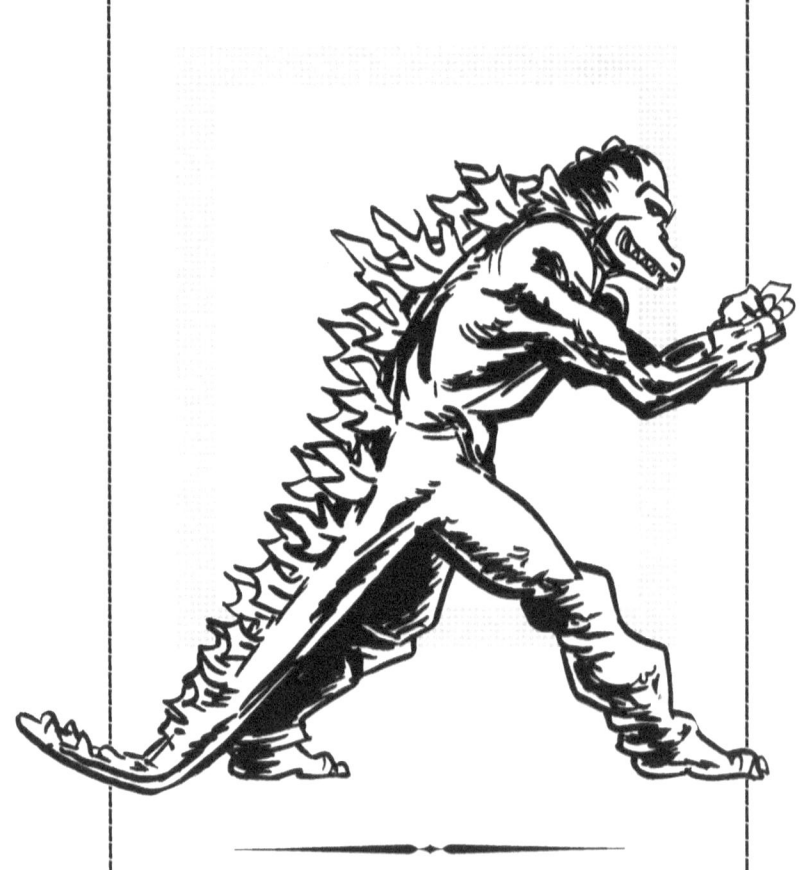

fig.9

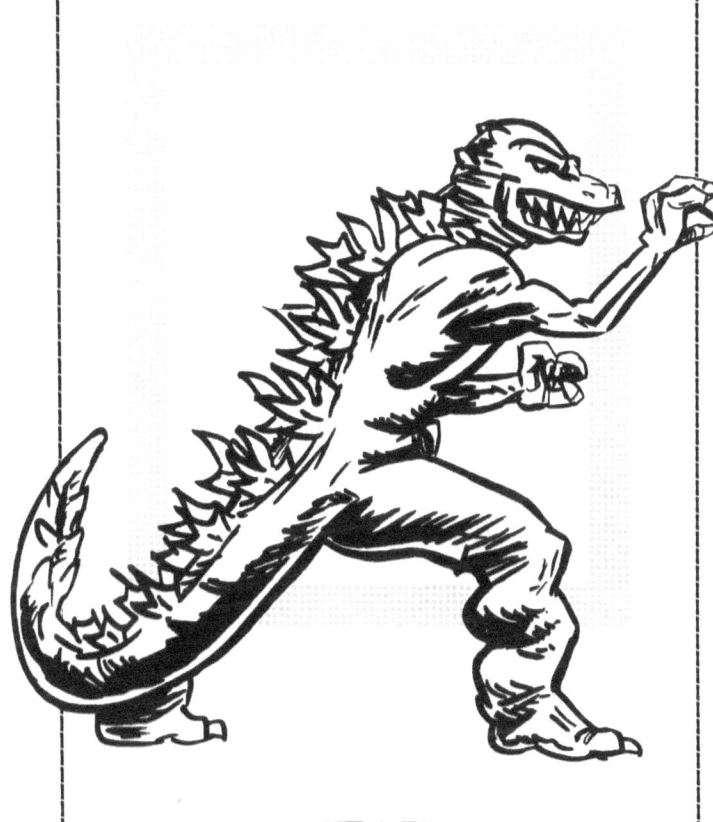

fig.10

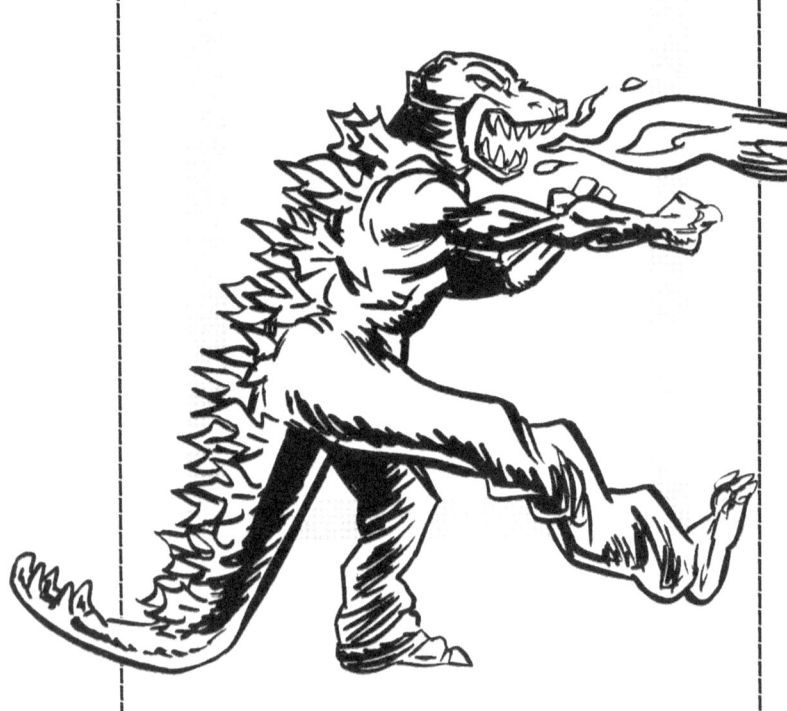

fig.11

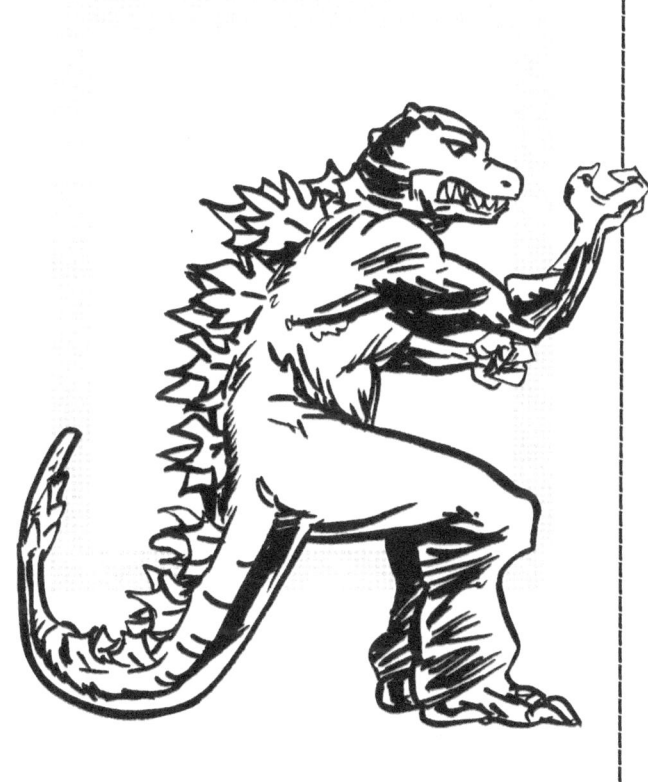

fig.12

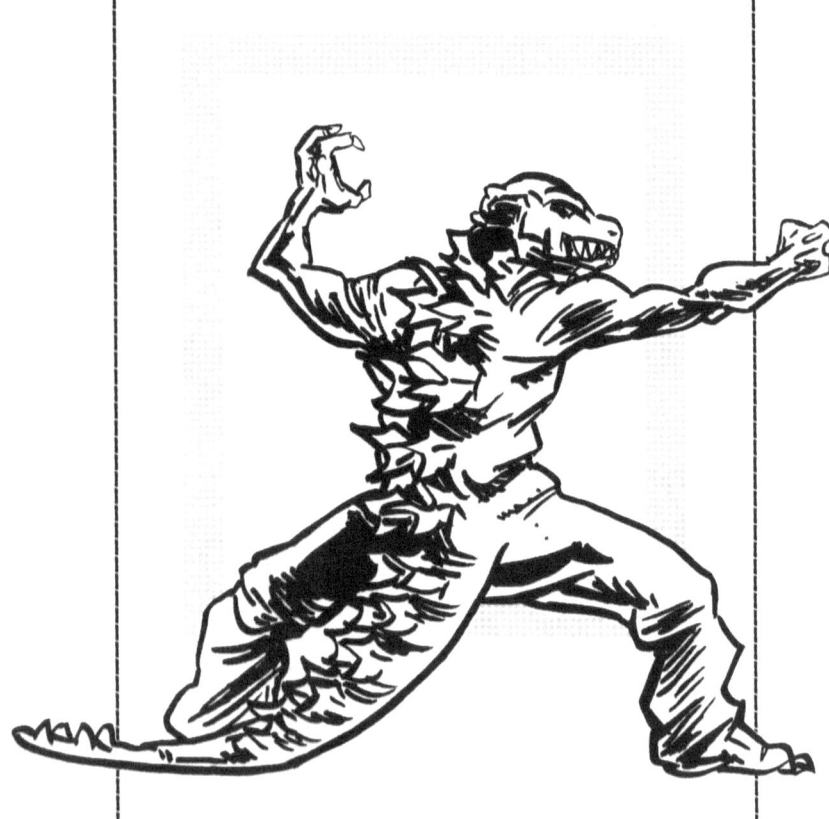

fig.13

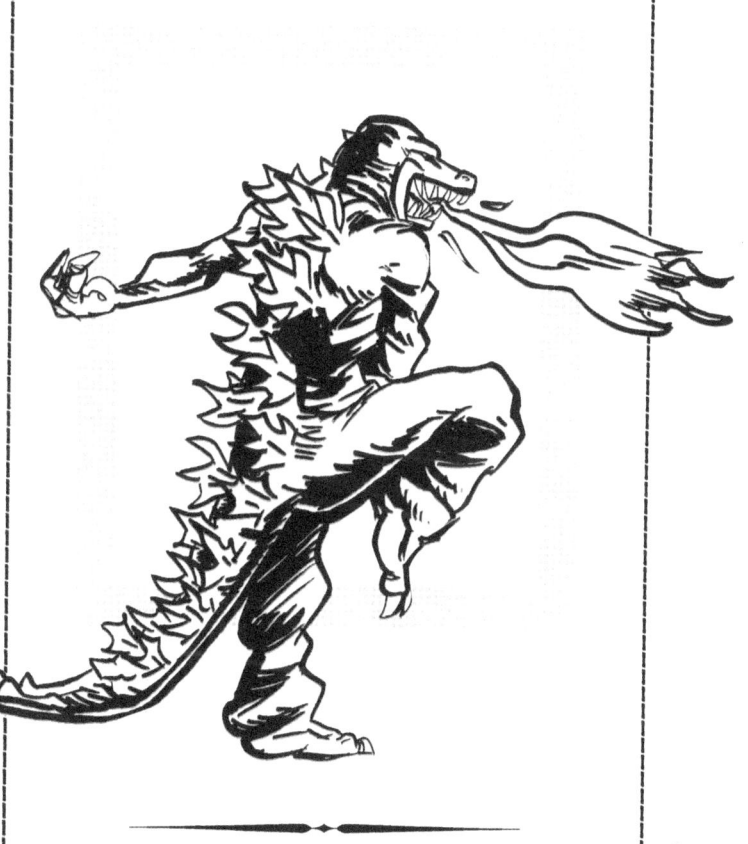

fig.14

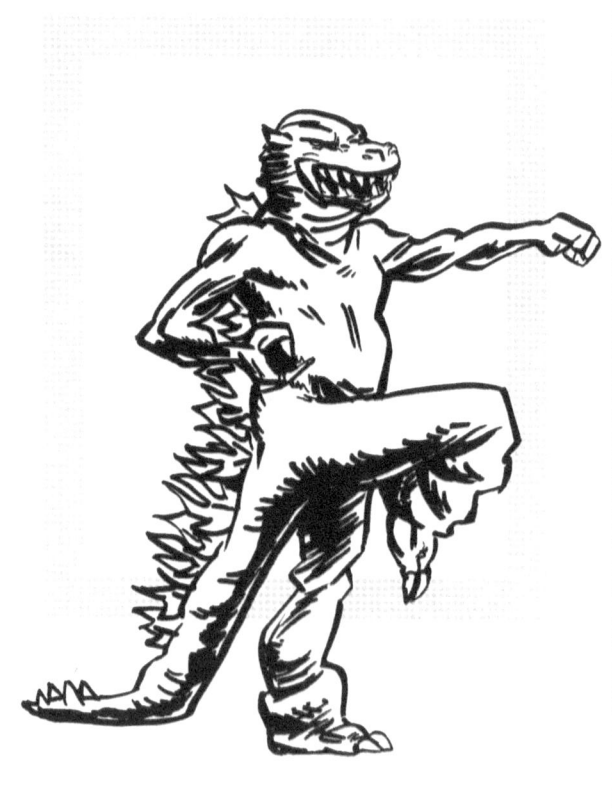

fig.15

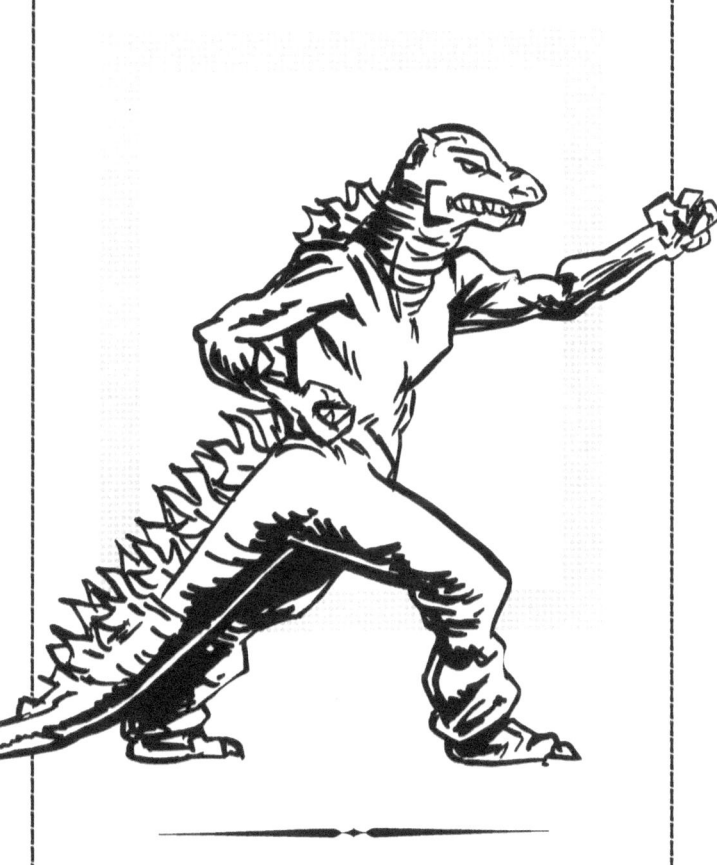

fig.16

APPENDIX I: We Have No Mantis Fist Diagrams

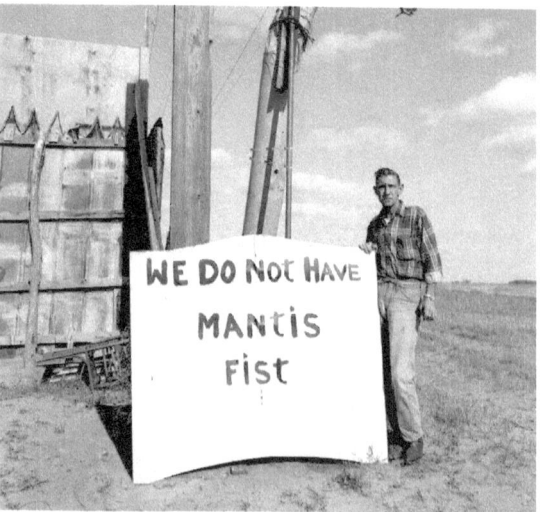

Image by Andrew Nahem

On 16 Dec. 2013, it began.

@Fisty: Hey @CulturalGutter Do you have any Mantis Fist Diagrams or the Manual for the Great Solar Stance?

@Fisty: But you have manuals, I know you do. Sacred scrolls, whatever. GIMME RT

@CulturalGutter: We have no kung fu diagrams!

@CulturalGutter: And none that demonstrate the

Great Solar Stance, so stay out of the catacombs! RT
@lowdudgeon: No bas-reliefs?! The hell, man? @fisty
@Fisty: I'll believe it when I see it!
@Fisty: Open the catacombs!
@lowdudgeon: OPEN THE CATACOMBS,
@CulturalGutter!!
@lowdudgeon: Deep below the Cultural Gutter HQ
lie the catacombs where they keep the micromosaics
and encaustic Kung Fu diagrams.
@Fisty: Here there be metopes, friezes, murals, mosaics, codices, and scrolls--and they shall be revealed!
@lowdudgeon: The Hall of the Gilded Vault is
dominated by the magnificent Mantis Fist frescoes.
@fisty @CulturalGutter #OpenTheCatacombs
#FreeMantisFist
@CulturalGutter: @lowdudgeon @fisty The
catacombs serve as a final resting place for The
Editors Who Came Before Us. Do not disturb their
rest!
@CulturalGutter: @lowdudgeon @fisty There's just
old skiing equipment in the Hall of the Gilded Vault.

On 5 Jan. 2014, it began again.
@lowdudgeon: @CulturalGutter Do you have Mantis
Fist Diagrams?
@CulturalGutter: @lowdudgeon We have no kung fu
diagrams, manuals or scrolls!

@CulturalGutter: @lowdudgeon We have no kung fu PDFs.

@CulturalGutter: Today's favorite search term: "manual arts best fighting styles"

@CulturalGutter: Today's favorite search term: "manual de kung fu"

@Fisty: @CulturalGutter Give the people what they want!

@CulturalGutter: @fisty No tenemos "Manual de Kung Fu!"

May, 2014:

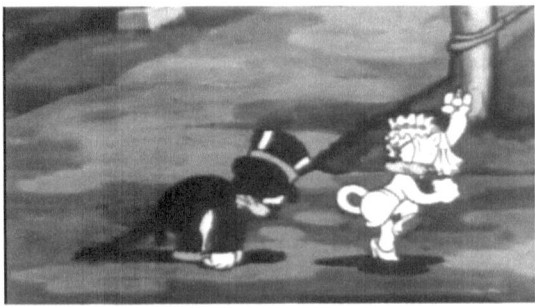

Dancing On The Moon 1935 animation by Max Fleischer

@lowdudgeon: @CulturalGutter @DriveInMob Is this what you mean by "tactical catsuit"?

@CulturalGutter: @lowdudgeon @DriveInMob It does look good for walloping.

@lowdudgeon: @CulturalGutter @DriveInMob Looks a bit like she's using Mantis Fist, too.

#HardToBeSureInTheAbsenseOfDiagrams

@CulturalGutter: @lowdudgeon @DriveInMob If only
we knew Mantis Fist...

@lowdudgeon: @CulturalGutter @DriveInMob The
sad lament of the Internet.

(As opposed to all those happy laments.)

@CulturalGutter: @lowdudgeon @DriveInMob
So true.

@Vulnavianist: @CulturalGutter Did you find any
mantis fist diagrams?

@Vulnavianist: @CulturalGutter So nothing on
Fistmaking with an Exoskeleton?

@HeidyMo: @CulturalGutter @Vulnavianist A mantis
fist diagram would be so bad a** though

@CulturalGutter: @HeidyMo @Vulnavianist If only we
had mantis fist diagrams...

June, 2014:

@CulturalGutter: Incidentally, there are only 1
Cthulhu Moleskine and 2 Homunculi left unclaimed
as Gutterthon perks.

@lowdudgeon: @CulturalGutter Not sure how to say
this w/o getting on your bad side, but I seriously think
a hilarious perk would be... Mantis Fist Diagrams.

July, 2015:

@CulturalGutter: Today's favorite search term: "Teach me kung fu"

@CulturalGutter: Today's favorite search term: "teacher of kung fu book"

And August, 2015:

@CulturalGutter: Today's favorite search term: "kungfu style"

@DriveInMob: People search because they know you have the answers.

@CulturalGutter: .@DriveInMob We have no kung fu manuals.

@Cultural Gutter: @drfreex @DriveInMob Our kung fu manuals would be public if we had any. Therefore, we have no secret kung fu manuals

@lowdudgeon: Follow-up question? Yes, I was just wondering do you have any Mantis Fist diagrams?

@DriveInMob: Double secret kung fu! Formidable.

@DrFreex: It's probably accidentally glued to one of @TeleportCity's posts and will be discovered while steaming rice.

@TeleportCity: I tattoo all of my secret manuals on the rear ends of flirtatious ladies, as Lee Van Cleef taught me to.

@CulturalGutter: However, the Cultural Gutter has no kung fu manuals or secret manual tattoos.

@CulturalGutter: @DriveInMob We are innocent writers of great meekness just trying to meet our deadlines. No time for kung fu.

@DriveInMob: You cannot escape the troubled world.

@CulturalGutter: Just floating and playing the flute and writing. What do we know of Mantis Fist?

@CloudLilac: @lowdudgeon @CulturalGutter I heard you had Mantis Fist Diagrams, though. Pepe told me you have Mantis Fist Diagrams.

@CulturalGutter: @CloudLilac @lowdudgeon Pepe was mistaken, unfortunately. We do not have Mantis Fist Diagrams.

@CloudLilac: @CulturalGutter @lowdudgeon Pepe said he got some Mantis Fist Diagrams from you. Pepe said they were really good. He says you had lots more.

@Cultural Gutter: @TeleportCity @drfreex @DriveInMob However, the Cultural Gutter has no kung fu manuals or secret manual tattoos.

@DriveInMob: A ruse. You are obviously going to transmogrify into "Invincible Ypsilanti" and take over the jianghu!

@CulturalGutter: @DriveInMob Could one such as I do such a thing? Here I have been fooled again. My bag of sticky rice is mixed with plain rice!

APPENDIX II: Mantis Fist-Themed Kung Fu Movies For Your Viewing Pleasure

The Deadly Mantis, aka, Shaolin Mantis (1978)
dir. Lau Kar-Leung
Not to be confused with *The Deadly Mantis* (1957), which depicts the Atom Age threat of a giant praying mantis terrorizing North America, *The Deadly Mantis* (1978) features Shaw Brothers' Studio superstar David Chiang Dai-Wei as Wei Feng terrorizing no one. The Emperor orders Wei Feng to infiltrate the house of Tien (Lau Kar-Wing, brother of director Lau Kar-Leung), a dissenter planning rebellion against the Qing Dynasty and to restore the Ming Dynasty. The Emperor warns Wei that if he does not return with evidence against the Tien family within three months, his father, a court official, will be stripped of his position. If he does not return with evidence within six months, Wei's entire family will be imprisoned. And if he does not return within a year, his family will be executed.

Wei disguises himself as a scholar with no mar-

tial arts skill and catches the eye of Tien Chi-Chi
(Wong Hang-Sau/ Huang Hsin-Hsu) as she is
throwing her former tutor out of the Tien family
compound. Wong Hang-Sau is easily the most en-
joyable part of this movie for me. With the English
dubbing in the video I watched, she reminded me
quite a bit of Myrna Loy. Chi-Chi isn't much for
book-learning, but she like the looks of Wei and
convinces him to become her new tutor. Chi-Chi
is really only interested in showing off her kung fu
skills to Wei. He is suitably impressed, especially
once he learns that her grandfather is teaching her
his notorious Shadow Technique. But she does
like when Wei leans over her while teaching her to
write.

The Tien compound is very secure and Wei is
restricted to his rooms and the garden. But Wei
does discover a secret message proving that the
Tien family is heavily involved in the anti-Qing
resistance, but he can't get the evidence back to the
emperor. Unfortunately, Tien knows that Wei is
a spy, despite Wei's clever ruse of saying that he's
just out for a stroll when he is snooping around the
Tien's house. At a family meeting, Chi-Chi begs
her grandfather to spare Wei's life, claiming that
they are lovers. Tien and Chi-Chi's mother (Lily
Li) agree to let her marry Wei instead. But Tien

warns Chi-Chi that Wei can never leave the village. If Wei tries, he will be killed.

So Chi-Chi and Wei get married. After six months, Wei suggests that they go visit his parents in the capital. Chi-Chi keeps saying she will talk to her grandfather about it and then putting it off. Wei finally goes to speak to her grandfather about this trip himself. And so an alternate title for this movie could be, *Wei Feng Can't Win*. Aside from overstepping professional boundaries both as a teacher and as a spy, Wei has discovered incriminating evidence that could destroy Chi-Chi's family. Will he betray her heart and his own by turning over the evidence? Whose family will he decide to sacrifice to the emperor? And, most importantly, what tragedy will drive him out into the woods to seek to perfect a new style of kung fu by imitating a praying mantis?

Dance of the Drunk Mantis / Drunken Master 2 / Legend of Drunken Master (1979)
dir. Yuen Woo-Ping

Dance of the Drunk Mantis is the follow-up to *Drunken Master*, in which the famed master of Drunken Style kung fu Beggar So (Yuen Siu-Tien, father of director Yuen Woo-Ping) taught a young

Wong Fei-Hong how to hold his liquor and stand-
ing up for righteousness. In the sequel, Beggar So
returns home. During his absence, Beggar's So's
wife (Linda Lin Yang) has adopted a son, Foggy
(Yuen Shun-Yee) to help out. God knows how long
Beggar So has been away because he's believes
the fully adult Foggy is the product of some affair
in his absence. A proficient martial artist herself,
Madame So has been teaching Foggy, but Foggy
has trouble impressing his dad. Beggar So refuses
to teach Foggy not only Drunken Style Boxing, but
any kung fu, because that's what sifus do.

Beggar So has been sending money to help
Madame So pay for his debts. But he's been
sending them to a shady banker, Moneybags,
played by comic relief character actor, Dean Shek,
who almost always knows either snake or cat-style
kung fu. But Moneybags has not been upright in
his dealings and Beggar So and Foggy have a "conversation" with him. And by "conversation,"
I mean, "fight."

Meanwhile, in the North, a magnificently
eyebrowed master with the unfortunately trans-
lated name, "Rubber Legs" (Hwang Jang Lee) has
not only created the Northern Drunken style, but
combined it with Mantis Fist. He has headed south
to find Beggar So and see whose style will rule the

martial world. Rubberlegs ultimately tracks down Beggar So in a teahouse and they have one of my favorite kind of fights: the refined drinking fight. It's a variation of the refined scholar fight in which scholars pretend to admire paintings, vases or wines while secretly displaying their kung fu and trying to beat each other up. Beggar So is almost killed by Rubber Legs' terrifying Drunken Mantis Fist. Foggy distracts Rubber Legs and then flees with his adopted father.

Badly injured, Beggar So is unconscious for three days. Madame So sends Foggy for medicine and Foggy encounters a man in a coffin by the side of the road. This man attacks Foggy while using some form of Weird Medical Exam Fist. It turns out that this is Uncle Sickness (Yen Shi-Kwan), Beggar So's brother, who knows the So family's four powerful kung fu forms: "Sick, Book, Magic, Wine." While treating Beggar So, Uncle Sickness begins teaching Foggy kung fu.

Aside from Drunk Mantis, the film gives to the world the gift of "Sickness Fist."

Thundering Mantis, aka, Crazy Mantis (1980)
dir. Yip Wing-Cho

Mantis fist and just a wee bit of cannibalism team up in *Thundering Mantis* starring Beardy Leung Kar-Yan, Chin Yuet-Sang and Eddy Ko. Leung stars as Ah Chi a worker at a seafood shop. But Ah Chi's heart is not in the world of commerce and fish sales. He wants to be the best at kung fu and in his spare time takes kung fu from a local teacher. He has mastered Shrimp Fist, which he uses for reasonably righteous purposes like thumping members of the Jade Horse gang when they shake down local businesses.

The Jade Horse gang don't take kindly to Ah Chi's interference in their affairs and after a particularly bad fight, they get Ah Chi's sifu to renounce him. Fortunately for Ah Chi and unfortunately for the Jade Horse gang, Chi befriends a young scamp whose grandfather is, as is so often the case, a secret kung fu master. The boy and his Granpa Chow make a living as street entertainers, doing acrobatic tricks to thrill the local townsfolk.

Granpa Chow (Chin Yuet Sang) refuses to take Chi on as a student, but Chi studies in secret, because that's how it's done in kung fu movies. After a particularly bad run-in with the Jade Brotherhood, Chow relents and teaches Chi the most powerful kung fu, Mantis Fist. In retaliation, the gang brings in their boss, Hsiao Cheng (Ko), who is a master of Eagle Fist and displays great skill in killing pigeons released by his minions. Ko murders Granpa Chow. The rest of the Jade Horse gang captures both the boy and Ah Chi. Back at Hsia's lair, things go bad until Chi goes amok and takes a terrible revenge demonstrating the power of Crazy Mantis Fist.

APPENDIX III: Master of Infinite Kung Fu

*S*ome of the most frequent search terms that bring people to the Cultural Gutter are ones involving kung fu, kung fu manuals and in particular, mantis fist diagrams. We have done some investigating and believe that what is driving this traffic to the Gutter is this piece about Kagan McLeod's 2011 graphic novel, Infinite KungFu. *This essay was originally published by the Cultural Gutter on March 29, 2012.*

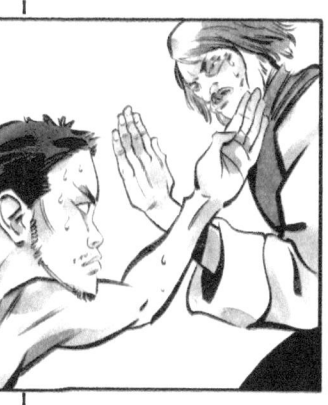 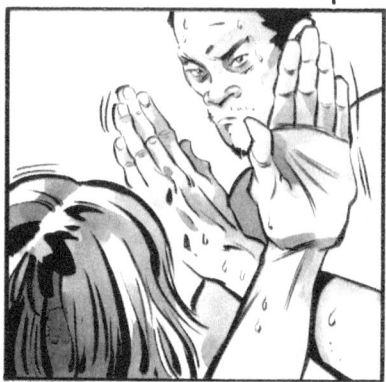

I always have trouble writing about comics that I think are good, just excellent and existing in their own seamless perfection, which means that here at the Gutter I don't always write about the comics that I love most. I want to do credit to them and save them till I have more time. Sometimes, I struggle just to say something beyond, "It's good." I've had that problem with *Infinite KungFu* (Top Shelf, 2011). Fortunately, the book's also gotten me thinking about action in a static medium and decompressed storytelling.

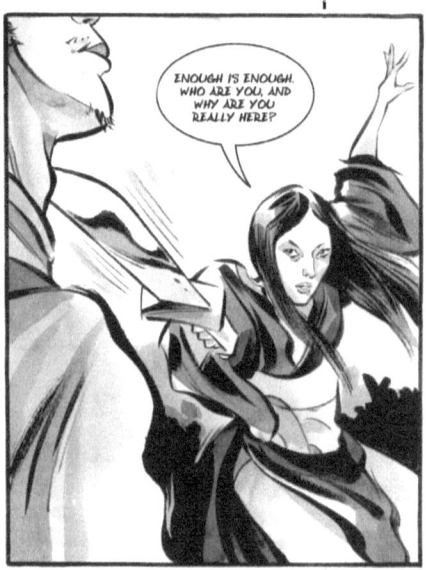

Kagan McLeod's graphic novel is a tour de force and like most masterpieces it's been a long time in the making. I got my first issue of *Infinite KungFu* at one of Toronto's late lamented Kung Fu Fridays screenings. Later, I heard McLeod was reworking it as a graphic novel. I impatiently watched Top Shelf's new releases and, finally, when the book was due to be released, it wasn't. McLeod wasn't finished. But *Infinite KungFu* was worth all the waiting and even at over 450 well-bound, well-written and beautifully-drawn pages, it's not too long at all. McLeod's lush line work, influenced by both Chinese calligraphy and Hip Hop tagging, would be worth it alone. But there's more. The Master Killer himself, Gordon Liu, and film programmer—and Kung Fu Fridays sifu—Colin Geddes introduce the book. McLeod also includes an essay, Brubaker-style,* on the history of Chinese martial arts cinema from the silent era to the present.

The book's set in the Martial World. In kung fu and wuxia stories, the Martial World/ Jiang Hu, is parallel to our own, encompassing a subculture of secret societies, itinerant heroes, martial arts masters and their disciples. In *Infinite KungFu*, the Martial World is beset by the risen dead. Yang Kei-Lung is a soldier serving in one of the Emperor of the Martial World's five armies, but finds his destiny when he encounters the chief of the Eight Immortals, Chung Li-Ch'uan. Chung chooses Yang as his student, tasking Yang with restoring the balance of life and death. There are also evil generals, secret manuals, Shaolin Bronze Men and a kung fu master based on George Clinton (Moog Joogular). And this kung fu comic culminates in an astonishing 84-page end fight.

I've written before about comics as a medium for the crazy mash-up. And *Infinite KungFu* does mix worlds, with Moog Joogular and his Funkadelic city grooving in the Martial World's midst. I've also written about comics as a silent medium and comics as a medium for horror. In struggling with how to write about *Infinite KungFu*, I started thinking about action in a static medium. It's self-evident, but in comics the movement, the action, the punches—whether Superman's or Yang's—are illusory. Yet, the most popular comics are two-fisted and action-packed.

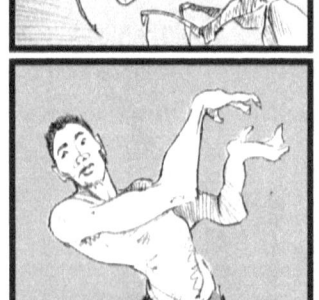

McLeod's gorgeous brush and line work go a long way in creating a sense of motion, speed and power. McLeod's panel layout and frames not only order the action, but elegantly emphasize a single blow's impact or a character's response. The book also features elements of decompressed storytelling, currently, the most common way of presenting action in comics. It's also called, "deconstructed storytelling," but "deconstruction" has particular connotations for me.

In decompressed storytelling, action is organized

cinematically. It's an attempt to create the experience of watching the story onscreen. A compressed story is usually complete within the space of 20-some pages. A decompressed narrative is usually complete within 4-6 comics—the number of issues collected in a trade paperback. A decompressed comic's space allows readers to admire the art. But when action is laid out as if it were a movie, the attempt to immerse me frame by frame distracts me because it makes a comic come across as a quick sketch of a film.

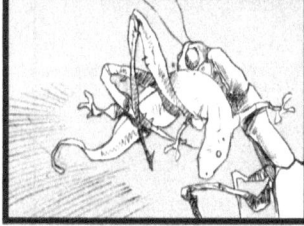
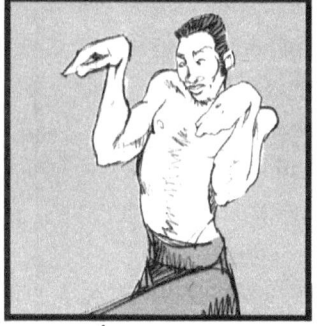

Infinite KungFu's final fight breaks action down into individual moves, but it doesn't seem cinematic in quite the above sense. And that's a little strange, because the book is all about a love of classic martial arts cinema. Maybe it's that McLeod uses decompression appropriately. After all, Shaw Brothers are right there behind Infinite KungFu. And McLeod highlights stances and styles in a way reminiscent of pre-1980s martial arts films, combatants announcing styles or pausing between sets of movements to allow enthusiasts to recognize, say, Mantis Fist. But the action reminds me of something else, too—the diagrams demonstrating stances in kung fu manuals.

Because Chinese martial arts are also a textual tradition using teaching manuals, kung fu has always existed in a static medium. Martial arts stories themselves are rife with secret books and prodigies with eidetic memories learning an entire style in a single glance. In fact, there is a long line of people with very bad or even no kung fu who discover secret books or carvings in a hidden chamber that allow them to become superhumanly powerful. In *Infinite KungFu*, Immortal Chung leaves Yang at the bottom of a cliff with piles of books. Yang can only stack them to climb back up again once he has finished them all. Yang's rival steals books of poison style kung fu and a secret Shaolin style and becomes inconceivably dangerous—and mad—from studying them.

In the end, portraying action in a static medium has advantages—and not just for mastering secret kung fu styles. In *Infinite KungFu*, it's easier to believe in the devastating power of the Emperor's Greater Yin Fist or a head hopping across a battlefield and onto its neck, because those depictions exist on the same plane, in the same style as everything else in that world. Unlike in a moving medium, they can't be undermined by bad special effects. Further, the creator controls what the reader does and does not see. The action in a comic depends on the creator's skill in rendering and on both the creator's and reader's imagination.

Between art and imagination, kung fu can indeed be infinite.

Ed Brubaker and Sean Philips include essays with their comics, Criminal, Incognito *and* Fatale. *It's a nice trend that's showing up in other creator-owned books like* Near Death *and* The Rinse.

Carol Borden regrets that she didn't buy one of Kagan McLeod's Bride With White Hair or Lo Lieh t-shirts when she had the chance.

Full disclosure: Carol received this book as a review copy. Kagan McLeod designed the poster for this year's ActionFest, the only film festival dedicated to movies that go BOOM! Kagan McLeod also designed the trailer for ActionFest, and Carol wrote text for it. Carol is writing for the ActionFest blog again this year. ActionFest's director Colin Geddes also wrote a blurb for the Cultural Gutter's book. But Carol's heart is untainted for they were all brought together by the love of kung fu and she would've written more about Infinite Kung Fu regardless.

Glossary Of Terms That Might Be Helpative

Chi or **Qi**. Some forms of kung fu depend heavily on chi/qi, the life essence that flows through everyone and everything. In harnessing chi, kung fu masters accomplish mighty feats from becoming impenetrable to swords, spears and, ideally, bullets with Iron Shirt Kung Fu (though that went poorly during the Boxer Rebellion) to seeming to fly with Light Foot Kung Fu. If chi is blocked by a clever opponent or through some misfortune, an unlucky person can lose all their kung fu abilities or might never develop them until the chi flows are cleared.

Ch'ing or Qing Dynasty (1644-1911 or so). The last emperor of the Ming Dynasty (1368-1644) had some trouble with rebels and bandits occupying Beijing and so asked his neighbors, the Manchus, to help drive them out of the city. Unfortunately for the Ming Emperor, the Manchus decided to stay and set up their own shiny, new dynasty, the Ch'ing/Qing. The Qing historically gave us a lot of

art from beautiful vases to China's first film indus-
try at the end of the Nineteenth Century and the
beginning of the Twentieth. And the Qing Dynasty
continues to provide us with kung fu cinema's most
pervasive villains. Even hopping vampires wear the
robes of Qing court officials. Kung fu filmmakers,
whether in Taiwan, Hong Kong or in Mainland
China have used the corrupt Qing officials as a
way to avoid censorship and criticize the govern-
ment, whether British colonial authorities or the
Chinese Communist Party, because even now, after
the handover of Hong Kong to Mainland China in
1997, everyone can get behind hating the Qing.

Kung Fu is most generally a kind of knowledge,
but in this case, it refers specifically to fighting
techniques. Different schools of kung fu teach
different fighting techniques often called, "stances"
or "fists." Many of the most popular fighting styles
in film are based on the traditional animal styles of
the Shaolin Temple: Tiger, Crane, Snake, Leopard
and Dragon. In both film and life, animal forms
proliferated until you can enjoy movies about both
Drunken Style Monkey fighting and Drunken
Style Mantis fighting. (Drunken Style boxing itself
claims its origins from the Shaolin Temple, which
decided that if monks were going to drink, they

might as well be able to protect themselves when drunk). Kung fu movies of the Seventies are particularly rich in audacious and diverting styles of animal-based kung fu forms. Characters frequently observe an animal and then combine a new animal style with techniques a recently murdered sifu taught them and then use this new stance to avenge their master or family or both.

Sifu. A master or teacher. A title of respect for a learned person.

Further Reading

Jean Lukitsch. *Electric Shadows: the Secret History of Kung Fu Movies*. (Red Lantern Productions, 2013) electronic edition.

Kagan McLeod. *Infinite KungFu*. (Marietta, GA: Top Shelf Productions, 2011).

Lisa Odham Stokes & Michael Hoover. *City on Fire: Hong Kong Cinema*. (New York: Verso, 1999)

Robert W. Smith. *The Secrets of Shaolin Temple Boxing*. (Clarendon: Tuttle Publishing, 1990)

Jeff Yang. *Once Upon a Time in China: A Guide to Hong Kong, Taiwanese and Mainland Chinese Cinema*. (Atria, 2003)

"The History of Praying Mantis Kung Fu." www. mantiskungfu.com/history_of_praying_mantis_kung_ fu.php. Accessed April, 2016. [Seven Star Praying Mantis Kung Fu]

"History." www.8step.com/mantis/history.shtml. Accessed May, 2016. ["Eight Step Praying Mantis Kung Fu"]

"The Legacy of Wong Hon Fan." www.chinwoomen. com/mantisboxing/wonghonfan.html. Accessed May, 2016.

About the Creators

Writer and purveyor of crazy talk. Maker of weird artsy things. Bringer of the wrong. **Carol Borden** is Evil Overlord and Comics Editor for *The Cultural Gutter* as well as the Editor of the Toronto International Film Festival's official Midnight Madness and Vanguard film program blogs. Her short stories have been collected in anthologies including the Noir series by the British Fantasy Award-winning press, Fox Spirit Books. Most recently, her story, "The Lost City Of Osiris; A Tale of Western Adventure" was published in *Piercing The Vale*.

Evan Munday is the illustrator of the novel *Stripmalling* by Jon Paul Fiorentino (ECW Press) and *DOOM: Love Poems for Supervillains* by Natalie Zina Walschots (Insomniac Press). Evan is also the cartoonist behind the self-published comic book, *Quarter-Life Crisis*, set in a post-apocalyptic Toronto, and the author of a Silver Birch-nominated series of novels for young adults, *The Dead Kid Detective Agency*. He worked for eight years as a book publicist for Coach House Books, and now does a variety of freelance publishing work (mostly ebook conversion), illustration, and sells books at Book City.

About The Cultural Gutter

The Cultural Gutter is dedicated to thoughtful writing about disreputable art. Comics, romance, science fiction, fantasy, genre tv and movies, horror, games all flow into the Cultural Gutter. We take trash seriously. Find us online at: www.theculturalgutter.com

www.ingramcontent.com/pod-product-compliance
Lightning Source LLC
Chambersburg PA
CBHW021038180526
45163CB00005B/2184